My First Book About

Nature

Felicity Brooks and Caroline Young

Illustrated by Mar Ferrero

Designed by Francesca Allen

Expert advice from Dr. John Rostron and Dr. Margaret Rostron

Contents

Usborne Quicklinks

To visit websites w   about nature, go to
www.usborne.com/q   st book about nature"
We recommenc   ing the internet.

What is nature?

Nature is all the living things on the Earth. Trees, plants, animals, birds, fish and bugs are all part of nature, and so are you.

squirrel

bird

There's lots to see if you go for a walk in the autumn.

fallen leaves

toadstools

web

Look for all the things that live on an old rotting log.

2

Make a nature table
These are the kinds of things you could collect to put on a nature table.

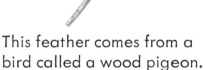

A snail lived in this shell.

This leaf may have been nibbled by insects.

This feather comes from a bird called a wood pigeon.

Moss is a plant that can grow in damp, shady places.

A dormouse made a hole in this nutshell.

These catkins are the flowers of a birch tree.

These are the leaf buds of a tree.

Pine cones come from pine trees and may have pine seeds in them.

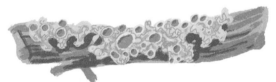

The crispy stuff growing on this twig is called lichen.

A baby bird hatched out of this broken eggshell.

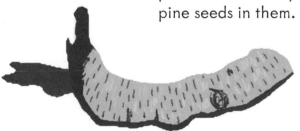

This bark comes from the trunk of a silver birch tree.

Nature's year

Nature does not stay the same all year.
Can you spot the things that have changed
in these pictures of the four seasons?

Spring

Summer

Match the picture stickers to the labels.

 hedgehog

 bird

 squirrel

 fox

Autumn

Winter

5

Plants and flowers

People grow plants in parks and gardens, but wild plants grow on their own. All plants need light, water and time to grow.

Here's how a dandelion flower grows from a tiny dandelion seed.

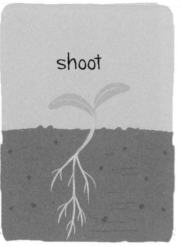

A seed falls on the soil. Roots grow down, the fluffy bit dies and a shoot grows up.

Lots of spiky leaves grow, and then a dandelion flower bud appears.

The bud opens into a flower. When the flower dies, a fluffy seedhead is left.

The wind carries the seeds off. They may land on the soil and grow into new plants.

Helpful bees

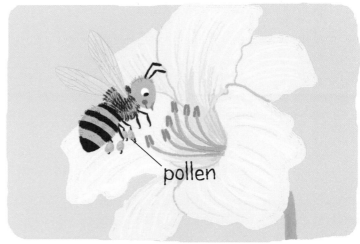

pollen

The yellow powder in flowers is pollen. Flowers need pollen from another flower to make seeds. Bees help them get some.

If a bee visits a flower looking for food, pollen sticks to its fur. When it visits another flower, some pollen drops off.

Here are some more wildflowers. Can you add some visiting bees?

common poppies

spiked speedwell

cornflowers

feverfew

white clover

7

A bit about trees

Trees are the biggest plants in the world and some are over 1,000 years old. Add the sticker labels to name the parts of this tree.

leaf

trunk

branch

roots

Changing trees

Evergreen trees keep their leaves all year. Others, called deciduous trees, lose their leaves every autumn. Add the stickers to show a tree through the seasons.

| Spring | Summer | Autumn | Winter |

Leaves and seeds

Trees grow from seeds and different trees have leaves and seeds of different shapes. Can you match the leaves to their seeds?

beech   horse chestnut   oak   maple

maple key   conker   beechnut   acorn

9

Kinds of animals

There are millions of animals in the world from tiny bugs to huge whales, but they all fit into groups.

bird

Birds have feathers, wings and beaks and lay eggs. Find out more on page 14.

cow

calf

Mammals such as cows give birth to their babies and feed them on their milk.

Bugs and insects are animals too. There's more about them on pages 16 and 17.

Lizards, snakes and other reptiles have dry, scaly skin. Most lay eggs.

insect

snake

frog

Fish and many other animals live in water. Find out more on pages 20 and 21.

frogspawn

fish

Amphibians such as frogs have soft, damp skin and lay squishy eggs in water.

What kind of animal is it?

Add the animal stickers to the page.

Amphibians

toad

frog

salamander

Birds

toucan

flamingo   penguin

Insects

fly

grasshopper

ant

Mammals

tiger

whale   sheep

Fish

shark

goldfish

stingray

Reptiles

slow-worm

chameleon

gecko

More about animals
People feed pet animals, but animals in the wild have to find food or hunt other animals to eat.

Some animals, such as elk, eat only plants. They are known as herbivores.

elk

Carnivores, such as wolves, eat meat or fish. They hunt other animals to eat.

wolf

Racoons are omnivores. They eat everything.

racoon

Food chains

A food chain shows who eats what.
We are part of some food chains, too.

An arrow from a mole to an owl shows that owls eat moles.

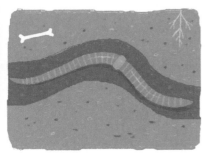

worm

mole

owl

grass

cow

human

What do animals need?

As well as food, animals need air, water, exercise and a safe place to live. Pets must get what they need from people.

Rabbits need clean water to drink.

Rabbits need fresh vegetables, hay and rabbit food to eat.

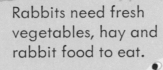

A rabbit needs space to run around and a clean, dry place to rest.

All about birds

Birds live all over the world and come in many shapes and sizes. Peacocks, eagles, flamingos and parrots are all birds.

The world's biggest birds are ostriches. At 2.8m (9.2ft) tall, they are much taller than grown-ups.

This is the actual size of a bee hummingbird, the smallest bird. It's only 5cm (2in) long from beak to tail.

Bird words

Whatever their shape and size, all birds have a beak, wings and feathers, and they all lay eggs.

Add the labels to this picture of an oriole.

beak

Birds grow a new set of feathers every year.

wing

breast

claws

feather

tail

Here are some birds that may visit gardens around the world.

pigeon

If you put some food out for wild birds, they may visit more often.

magpie

starling

goldfinch

thrush

sparrow

Baby birds

Many birds build cosy homes called nests from grass, twigs and moss.

A mother bird lays eggs in the nest. When they hatch, tiny chicks come out.

The parent birds bring food to the chicks until they are ready to fly.

Insects and bugs

Wherever you live, tiny animals are all around and many of them are insects. Over a million kinds have been discovered so far.

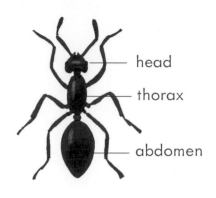

Insects have a head, six legs and a two-part body.

Add some bugs, slugs and other little animals to this picture. Which ones do you think are insects?

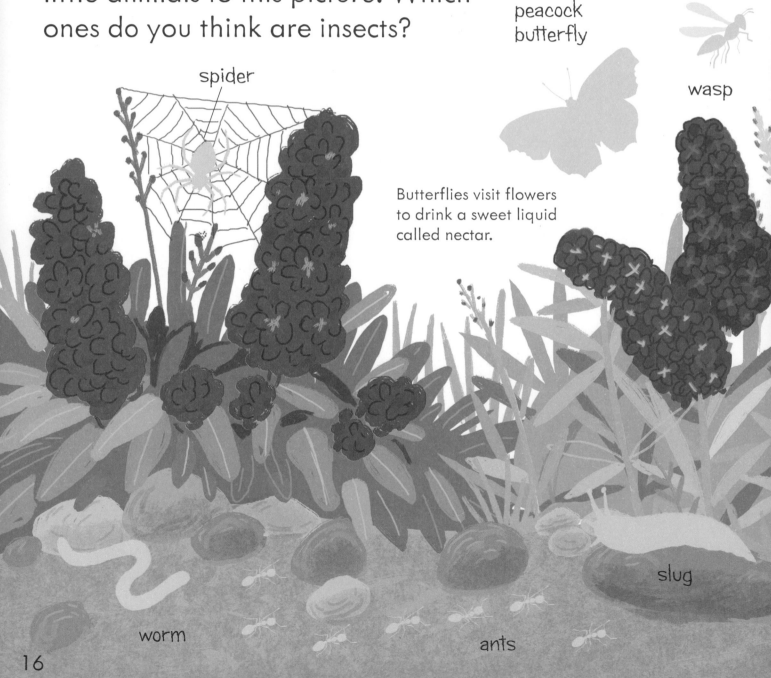

spider

peacock butterfly

wasp

Butterflies visit flowers to drink a sweet liquid called nectar.

slug

worm

ants

From egg to butterfly

eggs

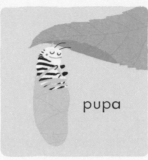

pupa

A butterfly lays eggs on a plant. Tiny caterpillars come out of them.

A caterpillar eats and eats and grows fast, then it hangs down from a plant.

A case called a pupa forms from its body and its skin falls off.

After a few weeks, the pupa breaks open. A butterfly comes out.

Butterflies, moths, ants, bees, wasps, shieldbugs, earwigs and ladybirds are all insects.

moth

shieldbug

bee

ladybird

woodlouse

snail

caterpillar

earwig

The deep dark sea

The further down you go in the sea, the colder and darker it gets. Different kinds of plants and animals live in each layer or 'zone'.

Add the picture stickers and labels to the pages.

All sorts of fish, dolphins and whales live in the sunlit zone, along with all the plants.

humpback whale

This is the twilight zone. It only gets a little light, but some kinds of sea animals live here.

swordfish

flashlight fish

hatchet fish

In the sunless zone, it's dark and the water is just above freezing. Only a few kinds of animals live here.

vampire squid

The abyssal zone is icy cold and dark all the time. Some strange fish live down here.

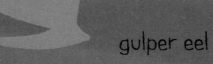

gulper eel

Seabirds dive into the water to catch fish.

tuna

dolphin

jellyfish

basking shark

turtle

This is a coral reef.

sunlit zone

squid

sperm whale

twilight zone

black swallower

cookiecutter shark

sunless zone

tripod fish

anglerfish

abyssal zone

19

By the water

Ponds, lakes and rivers are home to all kinds of creatures. Here are some to look for around a pond.

Add the stickers to finish the picture.

Herons visit ponds to catch fish.

heron

yellow iris

caddisfly

dragonfly

pond-skater

common newt

stickleback

Tadpoles and frogs

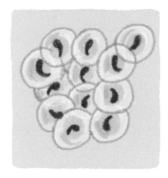

tadpole

frog

Frogs lay tiny eggs covered in jelly in water. It's called frogspawn.

Baby frogs called tadpoles grow in the jelly. Then they nibble a way out.

Tadpoles start to grow legs and then their tails get shorter.

Finally their tails disappear. Now the tadpoles have become tiny frogs.

greater reedmace

damselfly

common toad

waterlily

duckweed

great pond snail

great diving beetle

On the beach

When the sea goes out, pools of water are left between the rocks on a beach. Many plants and animals live in these pools. Here are a few you might spot.

Add the stickers to this picture.

seagulls

sea

sand

rock

limpet

periwinkles

seaweed

sea anemone

crab

starfish

blenny

Beach treasures

These are some things you might find on a beach. Which one shouldn't be here?

seashells

Razor-shells are long and thin. What other shell shapes can you see?

People sometimes call these cases 'mermaid's purses'.

egg case of a ray

These cases contained the eggs of fish called rays and dogfish.

plastic bottle top

A cuttlebone is the inside shell of a cuttlefish.

Sand dollars are animals similar to starfish.

sand dollar

cuttlebone

seaweed

driftwood

pebbles

Herring gulls visit the beach looking for food.

23

Animal tracks

Some animals have walked, run, or hopped across this page and left their tracks.

bear

Add the right animal stickers to the tracks.

horse

fox

rabbit

bird

mouse

Nature's year (pages 4 – 5)

bird   hedgehog

fox   squirrel

Plants, flowers and trees (pages 6 – 9)

leaf   trunk

roots   branch

bees

feather

summer   elk   winter

what kind of animal is it? (page   wing

ant

toucan

frog

racoon   beak   fly   tiger

grasshopper   flamingo   whale   penguin

shark

slow-worm

sheep

salamander

goldfish

stingray

gecko

chameleon

More about animals (page 12)

wolf

All about birds (page 14)

tail

breast

claws

Insects and bugs (pages 16 – 17)

spider

peacock butterfly

wasp

earwig

bee

shieldbug

slug

snail

ants

woodlouse

moth

worm

ladybird

caterpillar

The deep dark sea (pages 18 – 19)

swordfish

humpback whale

cookiecutter shark

jellyfish

black swallower

basking shark

turtle

sperm whale

tripod fish

tuna

anglerfish

squid

hatchet fish

dolphin

gulper eel

flashlight fish

sunlit zone

sunless zone

vampire squid

twilight zone

abyssal zone

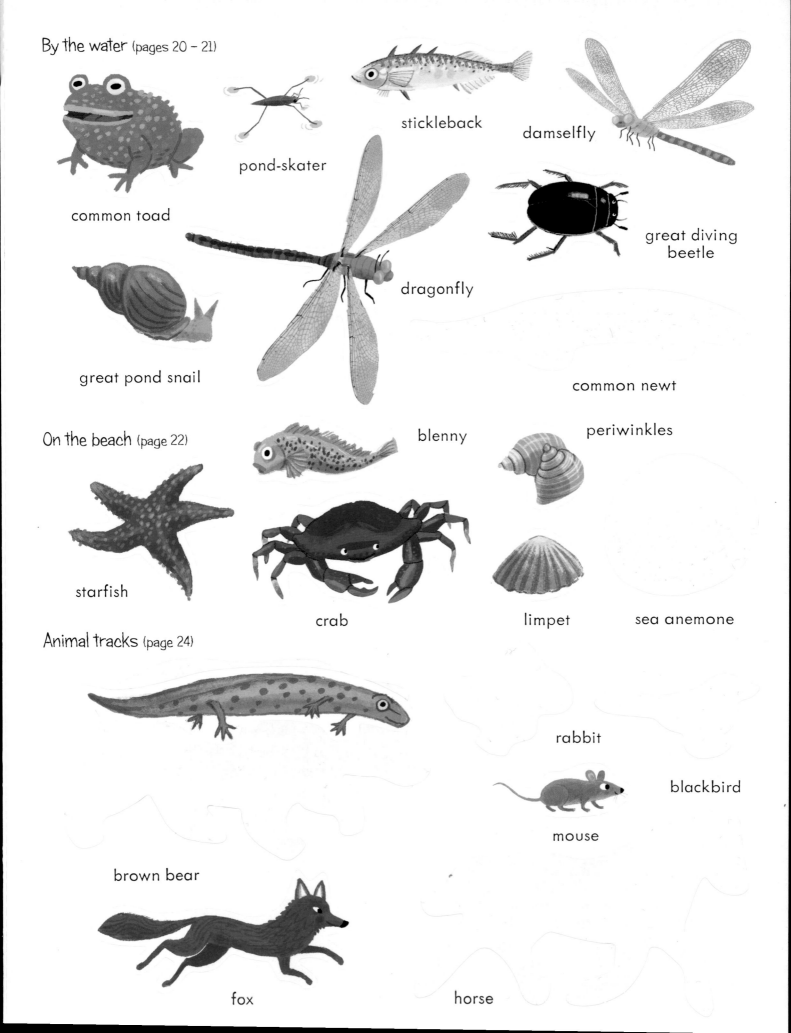

By the water (pages 20 – 21)

common toad

pond-skater

stickleback

damselfly

great diving beetle

dragonfly

great pond snail

common newt

On the beach (page 22)

blenny

periwinkles

starfish

crab

limpet

sea anemone

Animal tracks (page 24)

rabbit

blackbird

mouse

brown bear

fox

horse